Military Mom

Prayer Journal

ARMY MOM STRONG

Printed in the United States of America

Military Mom Prayer Journal

ArmyMomStrong.com

ISBN: 9781090428837

Introduction

While my soldier was deployed to Afghanistan, I spent the days and nights worrying and being anxious, wishing I could protect him. It was difficult to get through the day.

During that time, I turned to God in prayer and praise. My faith in God was strengthened as I learned to look to the Lord to protect my soldier and to help me be brave.

Many bible scriptures and heartfelt prayers got me through those times. By the end of that year, I was a stronger Military Mom and my relationship with God grew closer.

Spilling my thoughts and prayers into a journal helped me to embrace this Military Mom journey with courage and comfort, even in the tough times. I was inspired to create this Military Mom Prayer Journal to help you lift the weight of worry from your mind while your loved one serves.

This *Military Mom Prayer Journal* includes bible verses to encourage and give you the spiritual strength to rise to the challenges of military life. Each verse is accompanied by a lined page to journal your Thoughts, Reflections and Praise.

> *"So let us come boldly to the throne of our gracious God. There we will receive his mercy, and we will find grace to help us when we need it most." Hebrews 4:16*

I hope you will find strength, peace, courage and faith from the Bible verses herein as you journal your way to your best life and spend quiet time with God.

~Army Mom Strong

Worry
and
Anxiety

From Basic Training to deployments, worrying and feeling anxious were challenges that caused too many sleepless nights. These feelings were overwhelming and sapped all my strength.

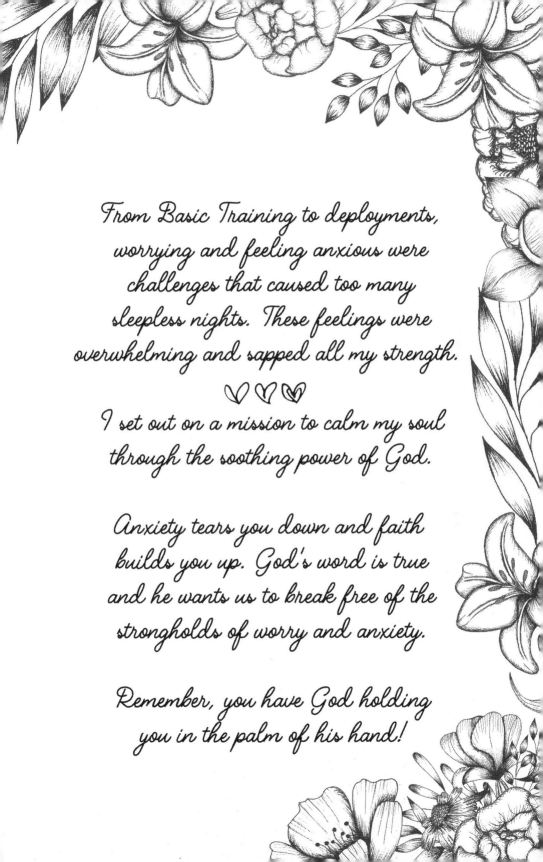

I set out on a mission to calm my soul through the soothing power of God.

Anxiety tears you down and faith builds you up. God's word is true and he wants us to break free of the strongholds of worry and anxiety.

Remember, you have God holding you in the palm of his hand!

Be joyful in hope,
patient in affliction,
faithful in prayer.

Romans 12:12

Thoughts ✣ Reflections ♡ Praise

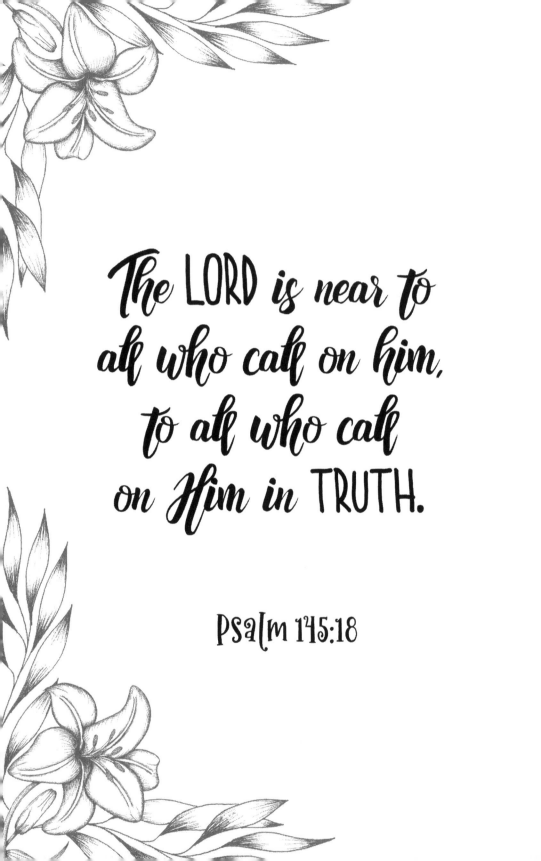

The LORD is near to
all who call on him,
to all who call
on Him in TRUTH.

Psalm 145:18

Thoughts ✦ Reflections ♡ Praise

Cast all your anxiety
on Him because
HE CARES FOR YOU.

1 Peter 5:7

Thoughts ✱ Reflections ♡ Praise

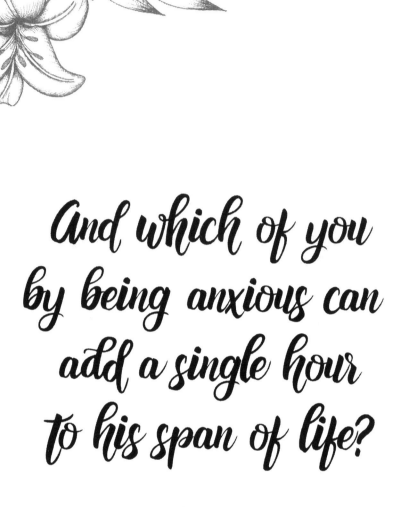

And which of you
by being anxious can
add a single hour
to his span of life?

Matthew 6:27

Thoughts ✱ Reflections ♡ Praise

Peace I leave with you;
my peace I give you.
I do not give to you
as the world gives.
Do not let your
hearts be troubled
AND DO NOT BE AFRAID.

John 14:27

Thoughts ✦ Reflections ♡ Praise

And God is able to bless you abundantly, so that in all things at all times, having all that you need you will abound in every good work.

2 Corinthians 9:8

Thoughts ✦ Reflections ♡ Praise

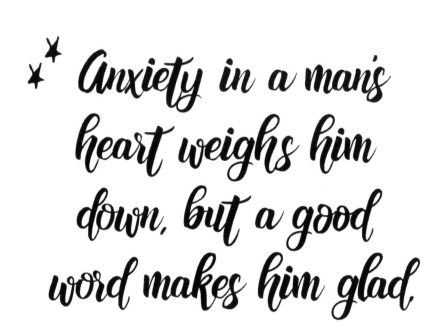

Anxiety in a man's heart weighs him down, but a good word makes him glad.

Proverbs 12:25

Thoughts ✦ Reflections ♡ Praise

I know the LORD is
always with me.
I will not be shaken,
for He is right beside me.

Psalm 16:8

Thoughts ✷ Reflections ♡ Praise

Humble yourselves, therefore,
under Gods mighty hand,
that he may lift
you up in due time.

1 Peter 5:6

Thoughts ✻ Reflections ♡ Praise

When anxiety was
great within me,
your consolation
brought me JOY.

Psalm 94:19

Thoughts ✴ Reflections ♡ Praise

When my son deployed to Afghanistan, I was overwhelmed at the thought of the dangers he faced. I was lost without the strength and courage to face the roller coaster of emotions we all go through while our children serve.

♡ ♡ ♡

I found courage and the strength to be brave through faith in God.

God's word is true. He can get you through these times and arm you with strength and wonderful blessings.

Trust in Him at all times, you people; pour out your hearts to him, for GOD IS OUR REFUGE.

Psalm 62:8

Thoughts ✴ Reflections ♡ Praise

When I am afraid, I put my trust in you.

Psalm 56:3

Thoughts ✱ Reflections ♡ Praise

For I am the LORD,
your God, who takes
hold of your right hand
and says to you,
DO NOT FEAR;
I WILL HELP YOU.

Isaiah 41:13

Thoughts ✦ Reflections ♡ Praise

Have I not commanded you?
BE STRONG AND COURAGEOUS.
Do not be afraid;
do not be discouraged,
for the LORD YOUR GOD *will be*
with you wherever you go.

Joshua 1:9

Thoughts ✱ Reflections ♡ Praise

I can do all things through him who STRENGTHENS ME.

Philippians 4:13

Thoughts ✷ Reflections ♡ Praise

May the LORD give
strength to his people!
May the LORD bless
his people with peace!

Psalm 29:11

Thoughts ✻ Reflections ♡ Praise

Fear

Giving in to my fears on this new and
unfamiliar military mom journey was
a constant battle that I faced.
Too many tears amid the fear kept me
from living my best life.
I knew that was not what
God would want for me.

Living in faith and not fear
helps me move past fear.

God wants to free us from fear.
Know that you can trust God
in all things as you grow your faith.

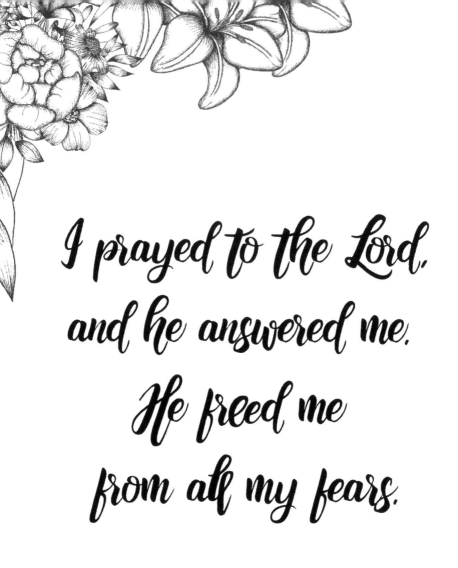

I prayed to the Lord, and he answered me. He freed me from all my fears.

Psalm 34:4

Thoughts ✱ Reflections ♡ Praise

He will not
fear bad news;
his heart is confident,
TRUSTING IN THE LORD.

Psalm 112:7

Thoughts ✦ Reflections ♡ Praise

For God has not
given us a spirit
of fear, but of POWER
and of LOVE and
of a SOUND MIND.

2 Timothy 1:7

Thoughts ✻ Reflections ♡ Praise

May the LORD
keep watch between
YOU AND ME
when we are
away from each other.

Genesis 31:49

Thoughts ✳ Reflections ♡ Praise

For he will command
his angels concerning
you to GUARD YOU
in all your ways;

Psalm 91:11

Thoughts ✱ Reflections ♡ Praise

Love

It's easy to get caught up in the emotional
ups and downs of life as a military mom.
Getting stressed or having a bad day were
becoming all too common in my life.
Being uplifting to others was hard, especially
when I had a rough day. It was easy
to set up walls and not let others in.

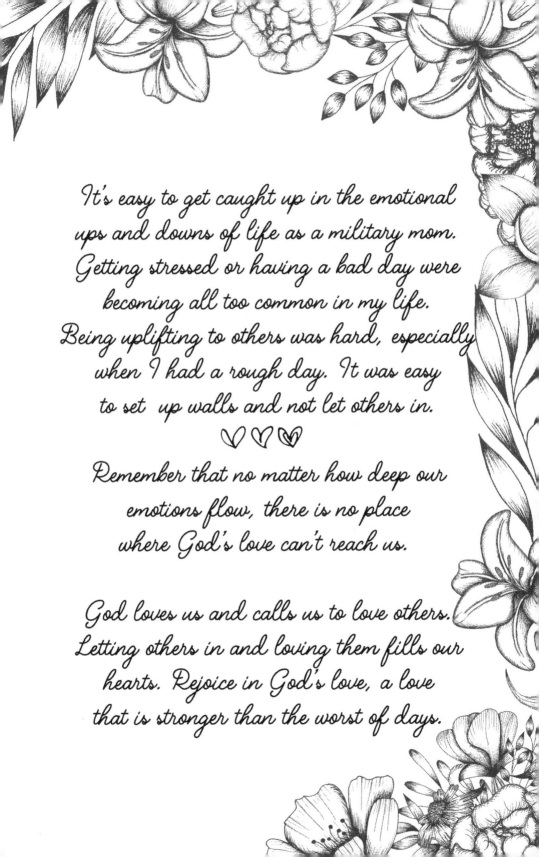

Remember that no matter how deep our
emotions flow, there is no place
where God's love can't reach us.

God loves us and calls us to love others.
Letting others in and loving them fills our
hearts. Rejoice in God's love, a love
that is stronger than the worst of days.

And now these three remain:
FAITH, HOPE and LOVE.
But the greatest
of these is LOVE.

1 Corinthians 13:13

Thoughts ✷ Reflections ♡ Praise

A friend loveth
AT ALL TIMES:
And a brother
is born for adversity.

Proverbs 17:17

Thoughts ✱ Reflections ♡ Praise

Give thanks to
the Lord, for he is good;
his LOVE ENDURES FOREVER.

1 Chronicles 16:34

Thoughts ✦ Reflections ♡ Praise

But you, O Lord,
are a compassionate
and gracious God,
slow to anger, abounding
in love and faithfulness

Psalm 86:15

Thoughts ✱ Reflections ♡ Praise

Be completely humble
and gentle; be patient,
bearing with
one another in LOVE.

Ephesians 4:2

Thoughts ✷ Reflections ♡ Praise

Letting Go

I remember when my son left for Army Basic Combat training. I cried at the airport holding onto a heavy heart. My most challenging assignment was to be working through the first steps of this military mom journey. I didn't know what to expect and had a tough time letting go.

Letting go of our children to military service can create new levels of emotion that we aren't prepared for. When your child joins the military feeling the weight of waiting for that first phone can keep you chained to your worries while stealing away your joy.

Know that God is faithful to us and our children. Pray for them while placing them in God's loving hands as you both begin this new season of life.

Do not be anxious about anything, but in everything by prayer and supplication with thanksgiving let your requests be made known to God

Philippians 4:6

Thoughts ✻ Reflections ♡ Praise

And we know that
for those who LOVE GOD
all things work together
for good, for those who
are called according
to HIS PURPOSE.

Romans 8:28

Thoughts ✱ Reflections ♡ Praise

And the PEACE OF GOD, which surpasses all understanding, will guard your hearts and your minds in Christ Jesus.

Philippians 4:7

Thoughts ✦ Reflections ♡ Praise

Trust in the Lord with all your heart and lean not on your own understanding.

Proverbs 3:5

Thoughts ✻ Reflections ♡ Praise

Protection

Being the mom of a deployed service member
had me wondering every minute of every
day if my boy was safe from the
widespread violence he was in the midst of.

This world was unfamiliar to me and
I often found myself down on my knees
calling out to God.

There was nothing to do except love and support
my son as I cried out with my heart to God
to keep him safe in the unsafe world he was in.

Stay in God's word and pray that he
give your service member the strength and
courage to do their job with a
shield of protection around them.

Trust in him.

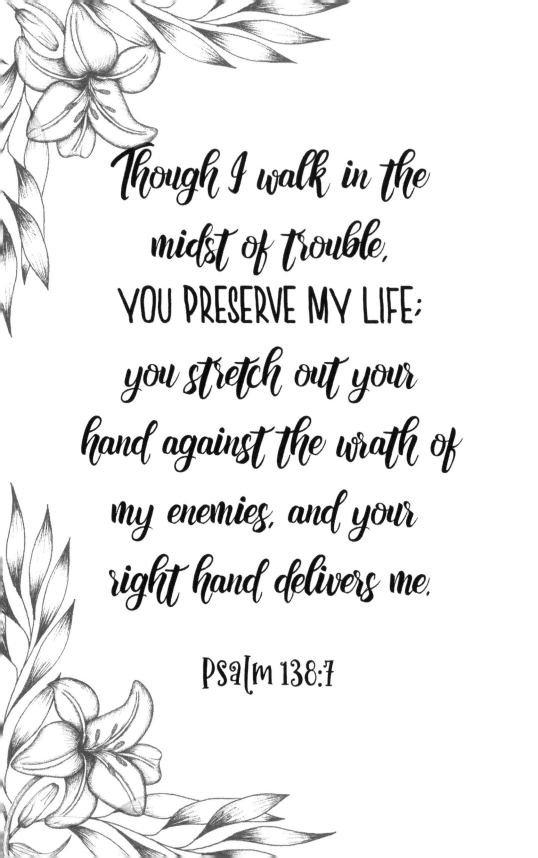

Though I walk in the
midst of trouble,
YOU PRESERVE MY LIFE;
you stretch out your
hand against the wrath of
my enemies, and your
right hand delivers me.

Psalm 138:7

Thoughts ✣ Reflections ♡ Praise

The Lord is my rock and
my fortress and my deliverer,
MY GOD IS MY ROCK,
in whom I take refuge,
my shield, and the horn of
my salvation, my stronghold.

Psalm 18:2,3

Thoughts ✶ Reflections ♡ Praise

He who dwells in the shelter of the Most High will abide in the shadow of the Almighty. I will say to the Lord, "My refuge and my fortress my God, in whom I trust."

Psalm 91:1-2

Thoughts ✳ Reflections ♡ Praise

Put on the
FULL ARMOR OF GOD,
so that you can take
your stand against
the devil's schemes.

Ephesians 6:11

Thoughts ✦ Reflections ♡ Praise

Even though I walk through the valley of the shadow of death, I will FEAR NO EVIL, for you are with me; your rod and your staff, they comfort me.

Psalms 23:4

Thoughts ✦ Reflections ♡ Praise

Those who trust in the
Lord are like Mount Zion,
which cannot be
moved, but abides forever.

Psalm 125:1

Thoughts ✷ Reflections ♡ Praise

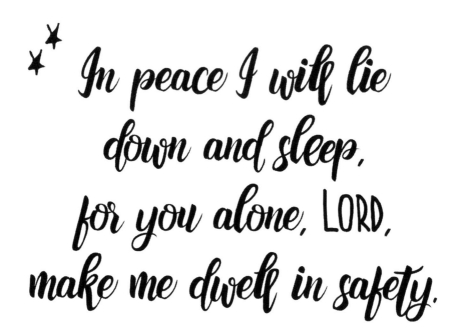

In peace I will lie down and sleep, for you alone, LORD, make me dwell in safety.

Psalm 4:8

Thoughts ✷ Reflections ♡ Praise

Peace and Stillness

Each new stage of this military
mom journey brought with it new
thoughts racing through my head.
It got really cluttered in there!
♡ ♡ ♡
I yearned for clarity, focus and peace.

I brought my burdens to God.
By fixing my thoughts on God instead
of the worries that occupied my mind,
my heart filled with God's love.

We can experience peace and stillness
by including a few moments of praise
and prayer each day.

Lift your heart and rest in God's presence
as you strengthen your walk with God.

He made the
storm be still,
and the waves of
the sea were hushed

Psalm 107:29

Thoughts ✦ Reflections ♡ Praise

Yes, my soul,
FIND REST IN GOD;
my hope
comes from him.

Psalm 62:5

Thoughts ✶ Reflections ♡ Praise

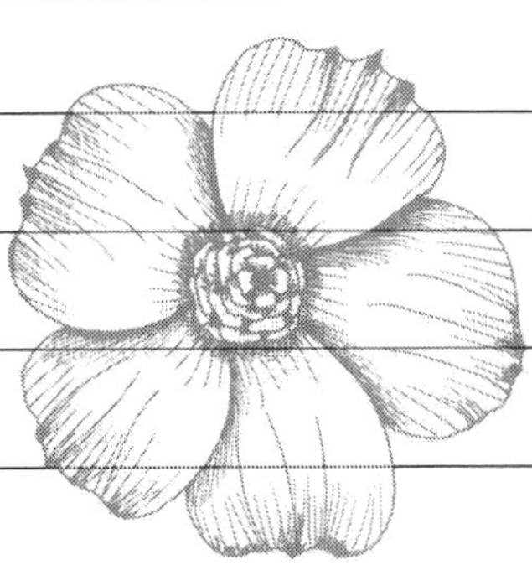

The LORD will
fight for you;
you need only
to be still.

Exodus 14:14

Thoughts ✶ Reflections ♡ Praise

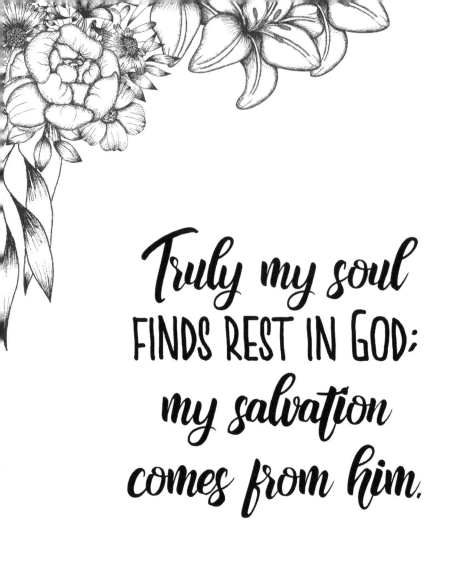

Truly my soul
FINDS REST IN GOD;
my salvation
comes from him.

Psalm 62:1

Thoughts ✦ Reflections ♡ Praise

I waited patiently
for the LORD;
he turned to me
and heard my cry.

Psalm 40:1

Thoughts ✷ Reflections ♡ Praise

Hope

Whenever my son prepared for an upcoming training or mission, I anticipated the worst and hoped for the best. I couldn't help but see him as my child who needed to be protected. My fears and feelings of hopelessness increased as my emotions grew more intense.

♡ ♡ ♡

Our God is a God of hope. I had to hold on to the hope that my son would be OK no matter what.

Looking to God is the answer to our greatest needs. Hope is encouraging and gives us the needed strength to keep moving forward. In faith and hope, we can turn to God for comfort.

His word has a promise of hope. There is hope when we trust in God.

For nothing will be impossible with God

Luke 1:37

Thoughts ✷ Reflections ♡ Praise

Give thanks in all circumstances; for this is the will of God in Christ Jesus for you.

1 Thessalonians 5:18

Thoughts ✦ Reflections ♡ Praise

May the GOD OF HOPE
fill you with all joy
and peace in believing,
so that by the power
of the Holy Spirit
you may abound in HOPE.

Romans 15:13

Thoughts ✦ Reflections ♡ Praise

*I wait for the LORD,
my soul doth wait,
and in his
word do I HOPE.*

Psalm 130:5

Thoughts ✴ Reflections ♡ Praise

Serving Others

At times on this military mom journey, I was so wrapped up in my own emotions that I forgot about those around me. By allowing myself to go down that path, I disrupted my relationship with God and put my emotions in a constant state of turmoil.

♡ ♡ ♡

Searching for a deeper purpose, I turned to God's word and grew my desire to stop focusing on me and instead, to humbly serve others.

God blesses us with a great sense of fulfillment through service to others. Living is giving whether it's volunteering, reaching out to a new military mom, education others about the military or just being a helpful citizen.

Strive to be a shining example to others through kindness and grace, as you give of yourself with a loving heart.

Each of you should use
whatever gift you have
received to serve others,
as faithful stewards of God's
grace in its various forms.

1 Peter 4:10

Thoughts ✦ Reflections ♡ Praise

Do not neglect to do good and to share what you have, for such sacrifices are pleasing to God

Hebrews 13:16

Thoughts ✴ Reflections ♡ Praise

And let us not grow
weary of doing good,
for in due season
we will reap, if we
DO NOT GIVE UP.

Galatians 6:9

Thoughts ✴ Reflections ♡ Praise

Whoever brings blessing
will be enriched,
and one who waters
will himself be watered.

Proverbs 11:25

Thoughts ✱ Reflections ♡ Praise

In the same way, let
your light shine before
others, that they may
see your good deeds
and glorify your
FATHER IN HEAVEN.

Matthew 5:16

Thoughts ✸ Reflections ♡ Praise

About the Author

When Lisa's son prepared for a deployment, she shed many tears amid sleepless nights. Feeling alone and unprepared, she scoured the Internet to educate herself about the mission over there, in a strange mix of fear and pride. Her search led her to found Army Mom Strong, an online Facebook community that supports and encourages moms of Army service members.

Over the years, she learned to find joy in this journey whether it be deployments, or overseas and stateside duty assignments, while strengthening her inner resolve through faith in God and prayer.

Dedicated to her family, Lisa enjoys traveling the globe for frequent visits with her family, wherever they may be. She is an avid runner, passionate about living a healthy lifestyle and helps others do the same.

Her adventures as an Army Mom over the past 15 years led her to create "The Heart of a Military Mom" and "Rise Up Military Moms" with co-author Elaine Brye to help inspire others who embark on this journey.

Learn more:

www.ArmyMomStrong.com
Facebook.com/armymomstrong

But the great thing to remember is that, though our feelings come and go, His love for us does not.

C.S. LEWIS